FOUNDATIONS FOR ABUNDANCE

LOVE, JOY, PEACE, PATIENCE,
PERSEVERANCE AND PROSPERITY

PETER J. DAHL

Foundations For Abundance

LOVE, JOY, PEACE, PATIENCE, PERSEVERANCE AND PROSPERITY

Copyright 2016 by Peter J. Dahl

Published by
HeartBeat Productions Inc.
Box 633
Abbotsford, BC Canada V2T 6Z8
email: info@heartbeat1.com
604.852.3769
ISBN: 978-1-895112-34-4

Edited by: Dr. Win Wachsmann
Cover photo: Jared Erondu http://www.erondu.com
Cover design: Dr. Carrie Wachsmann
Artwork and digitally created images: Dr. Win Wachsmann

All rights reserved. No portion of this book may be reproduced in any form without the written permission of the publisher.

Printed in USA

TABLE OF CONTENTS

Testimonials 4

Chapter 1 Abundant Life 9

Chapter 2 Spirit, Soul and Body 15

Chapter 3 The Exchanged Life or Great Exchange 19

Chapter 4 Repentance from Dead Works and Faith towards God Part 1 25

Chapter 5 Repentance from Dead Works and Faith towards God Part 2 31

Chapter 6 Foundational Teachings of Baptism 37

Chapter 7 One Nature 43

Chapter 8 Baptism of the Holy Spirit 47

Chapter 9 Renewing the Mind Part 1 51

Chapter 10 Renewing the Mind Part 2 55

Chapter 11 Extending Forgiveness 61

Chapter 12 Receiving Forgiveness 67

Testimonials

Peter Dahl comes from a biblical perspective, believing God's Word to be 100% true. God has used Peter multiple times to set people free from spiritual, emotional, and physical problems and to enter into the Abundant Life Christ promises.

Whereas many start from the outside, Peter always starts from the inner man, allowing the Holy Spirit to transform a person as God has intended from the inside/out. May God richly bless you as you walk through this series and experience all God has for you and others you come into contact with.
Dr. Richard Van Slyke
Founder Altogether Lovely Ministries
www.altogetherlovely.org

Peter exudes a quiet confidence in showing powerful life principles that are fully grounded in Jesus. Today, I can honestly say that I am a changed man, a better husband, a loving father and a strong believer because of Peter's faith in Jesus and me. I know I am not alone in saying this.
Quentin Harris

The principles Peter teaches are gifts from heaven that will enrich and encourage any life to a greater purpose.
Ann Marie Harris

Peter is one of the most significant godly influences in my life, and his Biblical teaching on Basics has had a great impact on me. So much so, that I asked him to come and teach Foundations (and other) classes at our church. As a result, I have seen God have a profound impact on many people through his teaching!

I regularly walk people through the diagrams that Peter shares in this material and it is a tremendously valuable resource that helps people see the truth of God's word clearly.

I have seen so many lives changed through this teaching ministry and I trust this book will be of great encouragement to you as well.

Cam Broad
Associate Pastor - Discipleship
Central Heights Church, Abbotsford

The Holy Spirit has used Peter to inspire and empower life changing truths in our life and marriage. We have found healing for the brokenness of our hearts by renewing our minds and putting into action what we have learned. We are enjoying an increase in our own capacity to receive the storehouse of blessings God has already given to us. It has changed everything!

Thank you,
Nicole & Rod Bradley

During the darkest and most painful experience of my life, Peter turned me around and pointed me to the healing power of the Cross of Jesus Christ. Peter also led me to the truth of continually being filled with the fruits of the Holy Spirit so that I could do all the good things that God planned for me long ago. I am now overflowing with God's love, joy, peace, longsuffering, kindness, goodness, faithfulness, gentleness and self-control, even when I hurt. I am God's saint, His precious Masterpiece. No journey through a dark valley can take God's love away from me and I like that :) Thank you Peter for having the courage to speak the truth to me when I so desperately needed it.
GC Bulawka

You are holding an extremely valuable and life-changing treasure in your hands! In June of 2000, while going through the most difficult circumstances of my life, I was thankfully introduced to Peter. Utilizing the very tools found in this workbook, he walked me through a process of personal and marital restoration.

No matter what obstacles you may be facing, the information contained in this workbook comes fully equipped to radically change your life!
Cory Dueck

A capsulated and rich Bible teaching and study guide. this unique presentation package takes you through an easy-to-understand, "straight to the heart" knowledge of who and what we are in Jesus. This presentation is packed with valuable information that is not only hard to find in one place but also quick to learn.
Karen Gerlish
President of *Haven Developments*

The Holy Spirit prompted me to seek mentoring from Peter while I was in my first years in the role of Women's Ministry Pastor. Peter's wisdom and direction for life and ministry transformed the way I thought and gave me a whole new freedom in my walk with Jesus. As my understanding of God's love and grace increased, I was able to mentor others and watch as God touched many lives. Leaders were released in their gifts and the women they served were changed by the power of the Holy Spirit. I am thankful for Peter's obedience in following Jesus. The passion Peter has for seeing others understand what God has done for them, teaching them how to grow and be released into their calling as disciples of Jesus, is truly transforming. I am thankful that Peter has put this material into print so that it can be shared with others and many will benefit from these words. Thank you Peter for your faithfulness.
Sandy Driediger
former Pastor of Women's Ministry
Central Heights Church, Abbotsford

Peter Dahl has been an amazing mentor to us. The Biblical foundational truths Peter teaches and his heartfelt care for us have led us each (and together) into a vastly different walk with Our Father over the last 7 years. Focusing on the unending promises of God, and how Christ and the Holy Spirit deliver on those promises in vast abundance has caused us to fall more deeply in love with God. This has empowered us to walk with confidence and freedom that He loves to partner with us in bringing forth His Kingdom!

Coming from a performance-based hamster wheel that often left us feeling that we could never "do enough", this freedom has compelled us to take a path of letting God show us how much He loves us, and that His Ways are always better than ours. The Paradox of the Kingdom is so very real on every level, and Peter's mentorship has given us the proper lens to see God's purpose for all of his children, one of abundance, more than we can ever wrap our minds around!

Dan and Tammy Kyte

CHAPTER 1

ABUNDANT LIFE

"I came that they may have life and have it abundantly."
~ Jesus (John 10:10)

Abundant: more than adequate; existing or available in large quantities; plentiful; over-sufficient; profuse; rich; lavish; abounding; bountiful; teeming; overflowing.

Life exists on three planes:
   A. **BODY**   B. **SOUL**   C. **SPIRIT**

The Greek word translated "life" is **ZOE**, and it means "life in the *absolute* sense, life as God has it."
(Vine's Expository Dictionary)
Strong's Greek Concordance G-2222
***ZOE* - life**

1. Are you experiencing the abundant life that Jesus speaks of in this verse?

---

2. Examples of what God's abundance looks like from Jesus' life on Earth:

A. Read John 2:1-11. Jesus turns water to wine at the Wedding.

v. 6 And there were set there six waterpots of stone, after the manner of the purifying of the Jews, containing two or three firkins apiece. (KJV)

Note 6 at John 2:6
Scholars refer to a firkin as being equal to about 9 gallons. That would mean these six water pots full of water turned into between 108 to 162 gallons of wine. This illustrates God's idea of abundance!

B. Read Mark 6:33-44. Jesus feeds 5000 men plus their families.

Mental exercise: How much would it cost to provide the food for over 10,000 people?

This story is told in each gospel (Matt. 14:15-21, Luke 9:11-17, and John 6:5-14)

C. Read John 12:1-8. Mary (Mary was Lazarus' sister, whom Jesus raised from the dead) annoints Jesus with perfume.

This was a very lavish act of utter extravagance! It makes no economical or logical sense, yet Jesus approves of it.

3. Put yourself on the receiving end of each of these stories, and imagine, how would this feel?

How would this change the way you look at and live life?

_____

_____

4. Do you think it is something to experience now or to be deferred?

If we do not believe this is for now, we will struggle. Proverbs 13:12 tells us that *"Hope deferred makes the heart sick, but a desire fulfilled is a tree of life."*

Look up:

John 5:24
_____
1 John 3:14
_____
Mark 1:15
_____

Jesus came not only to save people from the torment of eternal hell when their life on earth is done but also to give them this **ZOE** life, or God-kind of life, in abundance. The life of God is not only awaiting people in heaven but is the present possession of all born-again believers in their spirits
(John 5:24 and 1 John 3:14)

5. The first half of John 10:10 reads: "The thief comes only to steal and kill and destroy."

What has the enemy stolen from you? (relationships, freedom, joy, financial, health)

_____

_____

The good news is that we have authority over the enemy!

Rev 12:10

_____

Matt 28:18 All authority was given to _____

Luke 10:19 All authority over the power of the _____ was released to _____

You have access to this **ZOE** life!

First, you have to give up your earthly life (Matt. 16:24-25, Mark 8:34-37, and Luke 9:23-25) to receive this supernatural life.

Second, you need to transform any thoughts, emotions, or actions that are contrary to the Word of God, which is life (**ZOE** in John 6:63).

When you line up your thoughts, emotions, and actions with the instructions of God's Word, then this ZOE life manifests in your body and soul as well.

6. Reflect and meditate – This means that you need to take time for this! Lie down, go for a walk, or relax in some other way, and ponder these verses.

Romans 12:2

John 15:16

CHALLENGE:

Address your wrong thinking.
When negative thoughts enter your mind recognize them and turn from these negative thoughts towards God's promises.
This is the meaning of "repentance."

CHAPTER 2

SPIRIT, SOUL AND BODY

Now may the God of peace himself sanctify you completely, and may your whole **spirit** *and* **soul** *and* **body** *be kept blameless at the coming of our Lord Jesus Christ. ~ 1 Thessalonians 5:23*

Review: John 10:10

Christ came to give life abundantly. His part was to buy it for us by his death, burial and resurrection. Our part is to receive it and possess it by faith.
   Peter J. Dahl

Our challenge is to understand how we receive it and walk it out in our everyday life.

We need to understand ourselves - how we were made and how we were made to function.

The Bible gives us the keys in the following verses:

I Thes 5:23   Hebrews 4:12

We are made up of three parts:

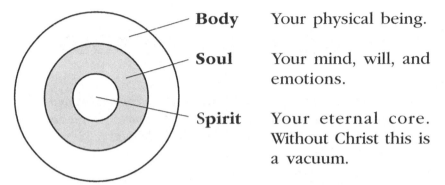

Body	Your physical being.
Soul	Your mind, will, and emotions.
Spirit	Your eternal core. Without Christ this is a vacuum.

The **Body** is the home of the five senses: sight, touch, taste, smell, hearing. It relates to the outside environment, the world around us. We are most familiar with that part of ourselves. Many of our physical problems can stem from "sickness" or "emptiness" in the soul and spirit.

The **Soul** contains our mind, will and emotions. With our mind we collect the facts; with our will we choose, with our emotions we feel. We really should not make decisions based on feelings; rather, feelings should come last, because if led by them, we often head "down-hill".

If the soul were a train, it would be wise to assign the mind as the engine, the will next, and the emotions as the caboose. We need to learn to first collect the facts with our mind, act with our will, and *then* let our feelings follow.

    MIND   WILL   EMOTIONS

The **Spirit** part of us is the part that goes on and lives forever.

Through our spirit we:

1. are...   Conscious of a higher power
2. seek to...   Communicate with that higher power
3. are guided by our... Conscience.
   It gives us a sense of right and wrong and will vary widely depending on our religious and cultural background.

When Christ enters our lives, the Holy Spirit seals our spirit.

    Eph 1:13   Eph 4:30   2 Cor 1:22

Write out 1 Thess. 5:23

_____

_____

Read it and note who is doing the work of "sanctifying" you.

_____

CHALLENGE:

What would complete life look like to you in all areas of your life? Ask God to show you practical ways this would work for you.

a) **Spirit**

2 Cor 5:17-21

___

1 Cor 2:12

___

b) **Soul**

Mind   1 Cor 2:16

___

Will   Phil 2:13

___

Emotions   Heb 5:14

___

c) **Body**

1 Cor 6:12-20

___

CHAPTER 3

THE EXCHANGED LIFE OR THE GREAT EXCHANGE

In this Lesson we want to talk about some BIG questions:
Why are we here?
What does it mean to be born again?
Why did Jesus come?

In the beginning God created Adam and Eve to be in relationship with Him.

He created mankind because he wanted family. He walked and talked with them in the garden. He also gave them freedom, which is necessary for any relationship.

They had to be free to choose, therefore there had to be something to choose instead of God. (Read Genesis 3) The fruit of the tree was this choice and it represented choosing to listen to another who desired to master them.

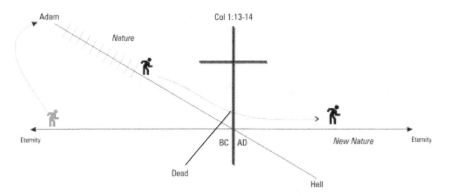

With their choice, they were removed from the line of eternal relationship with God to a place of separation.

With each passing generation, mankind continued to either turn their back to God or try to earn their way back to him.

God has continued to pursue mankind, as He desires to be in an intimate relationship with each one of us.

His ultimate solution was the Cross, where He did everything necessary to restore that relationship.

Salvation is God's idea. His desire is that all of mankind be restored to Him, as is evidenced in the following and throughout scripture.

Read these verses. How is God's heart evidenced in each?

John 3:16

I Cor. 1:30

_____

Luke 19:10

_____

John 16:14-17

_____

    New birth happens as an act of will responding to God's wooing or calling us and we invite Jesus to come into our life. At that time, his Spirit takes up residence in our Spirit. The two come together and create something new – a new you! 2 Cor 5:17

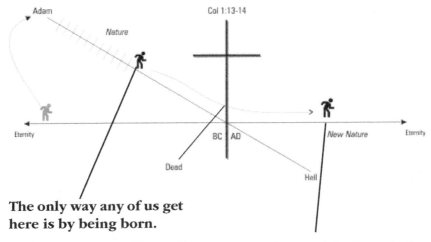

The only way any of us get here is by being born.

The only way any of us get to here is by receiving the gift of new birth (born again)

John 1:12 *¹² But to all who believed him and accepted him, he gave the right to become children of God. ¹³ They are reborn—not with a physical birth resulting from human passion or plan, but a birth that comes from God.*

Your part is receiving (believing and accepting) – ***believing is synonymous with choosing, not feelings***. God's part is to impart his spirit to reside within your spirit to create a new you. He also adopts you as a son or daughter mentally, emotionally and physically just as you are!

Remember from lesson 2 – God seals your spirit at this new birth and never leaves you. Read Heb 13:5 and 6.

What does He teach us that we can confidently say?

Ephesians 2:8-10 is packed with truths. Meditate on each part of this verse, asking the Holy Spirit to give you fresh revelation.

- Whose workmanship are you?
- In whom were your created?
- For what were your created?
- Who planned them?

Remember that this new life is to be "walked out."

Spend time picturing yourself walking these truths out in all areas of your life.

CHALLENGE:

Take time to thank Him for this gift of salvation and remember to say it each day until it becomes a habit.

CHAPTER 4

REPENTANCE FROM DEAD WORKS AND FAITH TOWARDS GOD

PART 1
UNDERSTANDING GRACE

Reminder: Repentance *is not a feeling*. It is a choice to turn away from believing a lie toward believing a truth from God's word.

The very first foundation in Hebrews 6:1 is repentance from dead works towards God. We must understand grace and peace if we are going to live with power.

Many people live trying to earn their way to God through good works: community service, giving time and money, reading the Bible enough, praying more.

While these are all positive things, God clearly spells out in the Bible that nothing that we do can make him love us any more or less than he already does.

Grace- God's enabling/empowering us to do what we cannot do ourselves.

Write out Ephesians 2:8 – 9:

_____

_____

John 1:12-14
12 But to all who did receive him, who believed in his name, he gave the right to become

_____,
13 who were born, not of blood nor of the _____ of the flesh nor of the will of _____, but of _____.
14 And the Word became flesh and dwelt among us, and we have seen his glory, glory as of the only Son from the Father, full of _____ and _____.

1 Cor 1:30
But by _____ doing you are in Christ Jesus, who became to us wisdom from _____, [b]and righteousness and sanctification, and redemption,

It is by God's will we are saved! The Father wants to have an intimate relationship with you.

Read Romans 5:17-21.

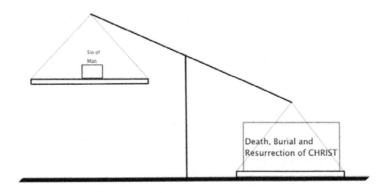

Which is bigger, the sin of Adam or the Death, Burial and Resurrection of Jesus Christ?

Think of your struggles. Did Jesus win that battle on the Cross?

(Go back to "What is the enemy stealing from you?" from Chapter 1)

_____

Gal 2:16 (KJV) *"It is the faith OF Christ, not our faith". Read that again, out loud.*

Notice the wording. Who's faith are we justified by? _____

Do our works buy us this justification? _____

Trying harder goes nowhere –

So ⬣STOP⬣ trying to do what you cannot, and embrace what Christ already did!!!

1 Cor 3:10-15. Good Works have a purpose with the proper foundation – only by the Spirit. What are our motives? Are we using quality materials to build on that proper foundation, ones that will survive fire? Where are we drawing our strength from? Like Paul did, remember to keep God's grace at the forefront, and His Spirit will give you the right tools and materials to build a life that brings Him glory.

With Grace,

there is *no* wrath left between God and mankind. What *is* left is His Covenant of Peace. If you are trusting in Jesus' work on the cross, you can be sure that only peace remains.

Now if you are instead trusting in yourself and your own decent life, then of course you can never be sure of peace. You can never be sure that you've done enough. But stand on Jesus' work, and you can be sure that *He* did enough.

Stay there. He did it **all. It is finished.** Wrath has been completely satisfied; 100%, and *complete* peace is all that remains.

CHALLENGE:

Look within and ask yourself if you have accepted God's Grace.
Have you made up your own conditions and terms that will somehow make you more pleasing to God, that will "help" Him to love you more?

Ask God to reveal to you any ways that you are trying to measure up to a standard that you or others have manufactured, list them on paper, and then prayerfully let them go.

Chapter 5

Repentance From Dead Works and Faith Towards God

Part 2
Understanding Peace With God

*"No longer do I call you servants...
but I have called you <u>friends</u>..."* ~ Jesus
John 15:15

We need help from the Word in dispelling our wrong pictures of God the Father, and how God sees us. It is very helpful to read through the Gospel of Mark and record how Jesus treated people. Keep in mind that **<u>Jesus only did what he saw the Father doing</u>**.

Read James 2:23

Do you see yourself as a friend of God?

Why was Abraham considered a friend of God?

His _____ was counted to him as _____.

What are some man-made or self-made qualifications for righteousness?

_____

_____

Even if you were to fulfill these self-made qualifications, would you see yourself as a friend of God? _____

**As it stands, we often don't see God the Father as he is - LOVE.
At times do you see him as angry? Fault-finding? Never satisfied?**

But John 3:16 proves that God actually didn't want to judge the world. He wanted to save it. Many people believe it is only the severity of God and his judgments that lead people to Him.

In reading Romans 2:4 we see that it is His first choice is for us to recognize His "goodness and kindness and to accept his gift of love and walk in obedience to live abundantly.

We often picture Jesus as saving us from an angry God, but in reality ***God was pursuing us*** in Jesus.

Look up these verses:

2 Corinthians 5:19
In Christ, _____ was reconciling the world to _____.

John 14:9   *Whoever has seen Jesus has seen the _____.*

Hebrews 1:3 *Jesus is an **exact imprint** of _____'s _____.*

God was behind it all. *God* was reconciling the world to Himself. What we see in Jesus, in His actions, in His words, in His emotions, everything we see is a carbon copy of what God is like.

We absolutely *do not* have an angry Father and a Son pleading with Him to calm down. Jesus said that looking at Him was the same as looking at the Father. What we see in Jesus is what we can expect to see in the Father.

Read Isaiah 54:9-10 and describe the covenant that we have.

_____

This is confirmed in the New Testament by Paul, who in Romans explains that *"Since we have been justified by faith, we have peace with God because of what Jesus Christ our Lord has done for us."* **(Romans 5:1)**

"justified" helpful. It's 'just-as-if-I'd' never sinned. So since we've been justified, 'just as if we've never sinned', since we've been made right in God's sight, we have peace with God because of Jesus. We have *peace* with God. He is not angry with us. He is *not* waiting or wanting to punish us. No, He is at peace with us.

With Abraham God called him a friend and talked and gave his plan for Sodom and Gomorrah.

Amos 3:7 *God does nothing in the earth except what he reveals to is servants and prophets.*

He wants his children to be aware of what is happening!

Read: Ezekiel 22:30

---

2 Cor 5:18

If anything is causing you to feel a lack of peace with God and how He feels towards you, this is not from Him.

So once again, this brings us to a choice. A change of mind. *Repentance*. It is not about "how you feel," rather it is about who you are going to choose to listen to.

CHALLENGE:

Read John 17:23
Take 20 minutes each day this week and meditate on The Father's love for you and your <u>friendship</u> with Him.

CHAPTER 6

FOUNDATIONAL TEACHING ON BAPTISMS

"For by one Spirit are we all baptized into one body, whether we be Jews or Gentiles, whether we be bond or free; and have been all made to drink into one Spirit."
The Apostle Paul (1 Corinthians 12:13)

The Bible teaches on three different Baptisms:

1. Baptized into the Family of God

2. Water Baptism

3. Baptism of the Holy Spirit

In Matthew 28:19 & 20, we have the famous Great Commission. We are instructed to *"Go therefore and make disciples of all the nations, _____them in the name of the Father and the Son and the Holy Spirit, _____ them to observe all that I commanded you; and lo, I am with you always, even to the end of the age."*

One of the first things we do with a new-born baby is to wash him. The prenatal life, as well as the birthing experience, has left its residue on the little creation that has been newly-born and requires a cleansing or washing. Parallel to physical birth, the first thing that a new born believer should experience is water baptism, which is the symbolic washing of our newly-born spirits. Washing is one of the words used for baptism.

What does the word baptism mean? Baptism is a transliteration of the Greek word baptisma, or baptizo, the verb. It means "to plunge under, dip completely under, or immerse in water." Baptizo was used in the cloth dying trade as the cloth had to be totally immersed as part of the process. The dye could never have been rinsed out of the cloth by a mere sprinkling. There is a Greek word for sprinkling, but it was never used in conjunction with baptism. All New Testament lexicographers translate the word baptism as "immerse," "dip," or "plunge." It is also interesting to note that nowhere in the scripture was water brought to someone who wanted to be baptized. They were always taken to a place where they could be completely submerged.

The first thing we are to do once someone has become a believer is baptise them, and then disciple them. However, we often try to change the order on this, and teach from a performance orientation. In our efforts to ensure the new believer realizes the full gravity of their decision, we encourage them to wait to be baptized. Although these good intentions are humanly logical, they are a subtle twisting of God's Word.

2 Chronicles 7:14 states that *"if My people who are called by My name humble themselves and pray and seek My face and turn from their wicked ways, then I will hear from heaven, will forgive their sin and will heal their land."*

The word "wicked" comes from the word "wicker", which means "twisted". We cannot afford to twist God's Word even slightly

> Baptism follows salvation – Scripture points to the urgency of this chronological order. The first occurrence of baptism was witnessed by the disciples and apostles.
>
> Jesus Christ was baptized, and He is our role model. After His baptism, His public ministry began. These nine biblical examples encourage born again believers to be baptized immediately! There appears to be an urgency to taking this step seriously.
>
> If we take the Word to heart, we will do well to follow the instruction to 1.) repent, and 2.) be baptized.

Read these passages and note the timeline of the baptisms.

Acts 2:41   Peter on the Day of Pentecost

___

Acts 8:12   Philip in Samaria

___

Acts 8: 26-39   Philip and the Ethiopian eunuch

Acts 9:17 &18   Paul's conversion

Acts 10:47 & 48   Peter with the Gentiles

Acts 16:13-15   Lydia

Acts 16:31-33   Paul and Silas

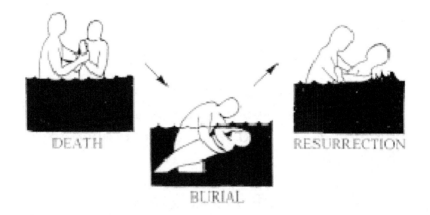

Symbolism of Baptism:

As we go under the water and come up, we act out the death, burial, and resurrection of Jesus. Baptism is also a visual picture of what has happened to us. We have died to our old way of thinking and living and are raised to walk in a new way of life, a Christian life.

We identify with Jesus through this experience. When we are baptized, we say to the world, "I am a follower of Jesus Christ."

These verses clearly point to the symbolism of baptism:

Romans 6:3-5

Colossians 2:12

Galatians 3:26-27

CHALLENGE:

Have you been baptized? If not, don't delay, and contact someone who has been a spiritual mentor to you and tell them you need to be baptized!

If you have been baptized, revisit what it means to your relationship with Christ.

If there are people you are close to who are waiting to get all their "ducks in a row" before they take this step, have a coffee with them and discuss what you have learned.

CHAPTER 7

ONE NATURE

"Unto the church of God... to them that are sanctified in Christ Jesus, called to be saints...
~ The Apostle Paul (1 Corinthians 1:2)

What defines you?

Do you see yourself as a Sinner or a Saint?

_____

2. As a Christian, do you see yourself as having two natures or only one?

_____

Many Christians do not really believe that the old is gone and the new has come.

Look up 2 Corinthians 5:17 and compare your answers

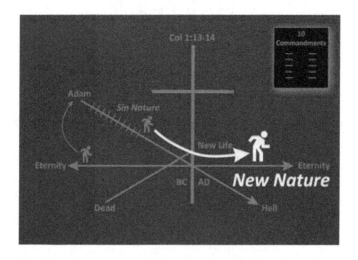

If we go back to baptism, we remember that it is defined as *"to turn up-side down in order to engulf and cover completely in fluid, having disastrous effect."* The "old self" has to die! That's a disastrous effect!

Many think that they have the sinful nature *as well as the saved nature*. The truth is we each have only ONE nature: either the "old" or the "new." Our one nature is either rightly or wrongly related to God. When Christ died for us, he gave each of us a new nature. This new nature could be accessed through new birth. Christ freed our will to choose to walk after the flesh or after the Spirit.

Thinking we have two natures is what I call being a schizophrenic Christian. The person who has this mindset, agonizes with trying to change from the outside–in. This is the opposite of what being "born again" is all about. This is like trying to change a dog into a cat by feeding it cat food and giving it kitty litter. True change must always come from the inside–out.

Remember the circles, with the spirit in the center, then moving out to the soul, and finally out to the body. With our soul, we choose whether to walk after the flesh or the spirit.

We are transformed by the renewing of the mind. How do we renew the mind? By being in the Word. When a person is born again, the Author of the Book comes to live inside – He is more than willing to give understanding of His Word when asked for clarity and understanding.

Ask, and you shall receive!

Only Christ is capable of actually living the Christian life; humanly it is impossible. The old nature has to be crucified with Christ. The old has to die and be buried, and then the new nature can be resurrected with Christ. To be saved is to be crucified with Christ.

Baptism is the funeral service for the "old nature," and the great celebration of the resurrection of the "new person." There can not be two natures living in the same place. The old has to go, and the new takes its place.

CHALLENGE:

Over 50 times in the New Testament, Christ's followers are called Saints!
Do a study and write down the references to at least a dozen of them.
Meditate on these verses and write a paragraph describing who you really are in Christ.

_____

_____

_____

_____

_____

CHAPTER 8
BAPTISM OF THE HOLY SPIRIT

I will ask the Father, and He will give you another Helper, that He may be with you forever; that is the Spirit of truth, whom the world cannot receive, because it does not see Him or know Him, but you know Him because He abides with you and will be in you. ~Jesus (John 14: 16 & 17)

The Spirit of God is with us to teach us, comfort us, lead us, show us Jesus, give personal empowerment and empowerment for ministry. All of these are the work of grace.

Remember that it is at salvation, in the baptism into the body of Christ, that the Spirit entered into you and is with you. In Acts 1:8, Jesus said "You shall receive <u>power</u>, after that the Holy Spirit is come **UPON** you."

The Greek word here for power is "dunamis", which has the same root as dynamite, dynamo and dynamic! The truth is, the power of the Holy Spirit is *explosive*, in action, and makes changes. We are to be in awe of this type of power.

Read the following passages:

Matt 3:11, Mark 1:8, Luke 3:16, John 1:33

What will Jesus Baptize us with? _____ and
_____

Acts 1:5 The Father has a _____ for us.

Acts 11:15-17
Peter was explaining to the Jewish believers that Holy Spirit baptism is for _____ and _____ alike!

Holy Spirit baptism is for _____.

A picture is often worth a thousand words, and it is easier to remember too.

Picture a bottle full of water. It is *in* the room. Let's say the water represents the Holy Spirit.

Now picture pouring one third of the water into a cup that is standing in a bowl. The cup has water *in* it. The cup represents the person, and once the water (Holy Spirit) is *in*, the person is born again.

At this point, the new believer is one third full of the Holy Spirit. Now picture continuing to pour water into the cup, until the water spills over the edges and overflows.

This is a picture of the Holy Spirit coming upon the believer, empowering that person to have an effect on those around him/her, spilling the good news over those who need Jesus. Some people call this becoming a fanatic!

The Holy Spirit coming upon releases the gifts that are already within.

In 1 Cor. 14:1, Paul encourages us to desire ALL of the spiritual gifts, which are vital for building up Christ's body, both individually and corporately.

2 Timothy 1:6 and Acts 8:17 give us the example of

_____

Being baptized or filled with the Spirit is something that is both critical and progressive, meaning that even if you have been filled with the Spirit and been imparted with his gift that it is something that you need to learn to walk in every day. If we do not understand this, it is so detrimental. Many of us have been taught that automatically after we receive Christ we live in victory, and yet the Bible teaches that our faith is a walk.

Read and reflect on what the Bible teaches in Romans 8:5-9 and Galatians 5:

_____

_____

Andrew Wommack teaches us that:

If Jesus couldn't, or wouldn't, operate independently of the Holy Spirit, neither should we. <u>No one can have an effective life or ministry without the power of God's Holy Spirit working in him or her.</u> This fact can't be argued by anyone who truly believes the Bible is God's Word. The Scriptures are replete with proof that it is "not by might, nor by power, but by my Spirit, saith the LORD of hosts." (Zech. 4:6)

CHALLENGE:

If you haven't ever asked the Holy Spirit to fill you and come upon you, consider approaching one or two others to lay hands on you to impart the gift of the Holy Spirit.
Be open to the spiritual gifts (prophecy, tongues, teaching, etc.) that He desires to build you up with.

CHAPTER 9
RENEWING THE MIND
PART 1

And now, dear brothers and sisters, one final thing. Fix your thoughts on what is true, and honorable, and right, and pure, and lovely, and admirable. Think about things that are excellent and worthy of praise.
~ The Apostle Paul (Philippians 4:8, NLT)

Everything that has happened to you from **conception** until **now** is stored in memories that have either **negative** or **positive** emotions attached to them.

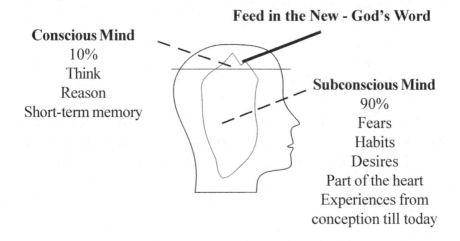

Conscious Mind
10%
Think
Reason
Short-term memory

Feed in the New - God's Word

Subconscious Mind
90%
Fears
Habits
Desires
Part of the heart
Experiences from
conception till today

If we focus on getting rid of the negative thoughts and emotions, we will be drawn to the negative and feel discouraged.

We need to focus on God's promises - learn to meditate on the goodness of God.

Meditate - haga (Strong's Hebrew #1897)
moan, mourn, utter, mutter, devise, imagine, speak, plot
Joshua 1:8, Psalms1:2, Psalms 2:1

A good example can be found in Exodus 23:29-30

Notice, it is a process. Little by little; a lifelong process of growth - being changed from one degree of glory to another.

A law of the mind is that whatever you focus on is what you will be drawn to and, in many cases, what you will become. For many people it is easier to focus on the negatives in life rather than the positives.

Because we are bombarded continually by internal and external stimuli, we need the Holy Spirit to help redirect our focus on God's Truth.

We need to make a decision to choose to let Holy Spirit fill us with the Affirmations of God's promises to us. In truth there are an astounding number of them!

Recommended Affirmations for Loving

1. I like myself unconditionally because I am a child of God, because God loves me unconditionally.
Ephesians 1:4,5; Jeremiah 31:3,4; Matthew 22:39

2. I enjoy the special and unique person that I am.
Pslams 139:13-16; Matthew 10:30,31

3. I freely acknowledge my failures and depend on Jesus Christ when change is needed. I never devalue myself with destructive self-criticism.
Ephesians 4:29; Deuteronomy 30:19; 1 Corinthians 6:20

4. The forgiving love of Jesus Christ penetrates into the very depths of my being and sets me free from the fear and mistakes of the past.
Psalms 103:11-13

5. Father, as your unconditional love flows through me from above, l give love and acceptance to all persons at all times.
James 1:17; 1 John 4:7

6. I can do all thines that are required of me today because through Christ I am strengthened, empowered and inspired to succeed.
Philippians 4:13; Jeremiah 1:12; Acts 1: 8; Joshua 1:5-9.

Meditation

Meditation has become a 'misunderstood' word for some Christians, because the church has let eastern mysticism derail one of God's main tracks to provide communication with Him.

Psalm 119:148 says: My eyes are awake before the watches of the night, that I may meditate on Your promise.

CHALLENGE:

Write out Ephesians 2:10,
personalizing it with your own name.
Then repeat it daily this week and ask God
to show you how you are His masterpiece!

_____

_____

CHAPTER 10

RENEWING THE MIND PART 2

Don't copy the behaviour and customs of this world, but let God transform you into a new person by changing the way you think. Then you will learn to know God's will for you, which is good and pleasing and perfect. ~ The Apostle Paul (Romans 12:2, NLT)

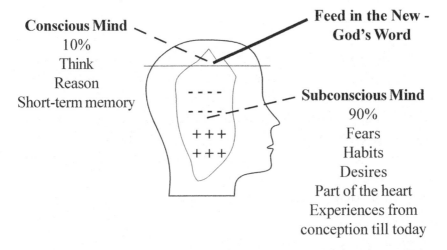

Transformation comes with the renewing of the mind. New information based on the truth of the Word of God needs to have access to the mind. As the new information becomes familiar, it begins to transform the mind. These positive thoughts, attitudes and mindsets build up, and push the negative and false thoughts, attitudes, and mindsets to the surface.

Ninety percent of our thoughts, attitudes, and mindsets are subconscious. We have developed them from conception through to the present day.

They shape our life. We think and reason with our conscious mind, which makes up the left over 10%.

A child knows from a very young age whether he/she is rejected or loved, and that person's self-image is established accordingly! It is imperative to deal with the negatives, replacing them with positive truths from God's Word.

We are to ***resist the devil and he will flee*** from us (James 4:7).

God came to set the captives free. <u>It was God's idea to set us free.</u> He paid the price. If there is garbage in our subconscious minds that needs to be cleaned up in our lives, God will reveal it so that He can free us of it. He wants to clean up our hearts and our minds. He knows that we generally do not know what to do with the intimidating and ugly garbage. He knows that we tend to stuff it down, ignoring it and hoping it will just "go away."

People often want the instant or quick fix. By chasing after a quick fix we often think that a one-time "deliverance" can solve everything. Rather, if we let it, God's Word will methodically push the garbage to the surface, and little by little, from one degree of glory to another, victory is won.

Walking in the Spirit - Seeing the Big Picture

A gold miner typically only mines a third of an ounce of gold per one tonne of earth. Instead of getting discouraged and giving up because of the slow progress, the miner rejoices over the little nugget of gold, valuing its worth. The miner sees the big picture, and visualizes a great number of nuggets adding up.

Tenacity, persistence, and focus on the growth instead of the size of the nugget give the miner a sense of accomplishment, joy and hope. In other words, the miner does not compare his progress to anyone else, but faithfully plods along.

Similarly, in learning to walk in the Spirit, we should celebrate the nuggets of truth that speak to our hearts, and learn to apply them in our daily lives. Little by little, we grow and experience victory upon victory. Instead of getting overwhelmed by the whole picture, focus in on what the Spirit is gently pointing out to you. He will never place more on you than you can handle.

In fact, the Word says that His burden is light, and that we can cast all of our cares and burdens on Him. He will take you step by step into a deeper relationship with Him. The Holy Spirit is not just a force or a power; He is a person with a personality. He is our patient and faithful Teacher and Guide, and desires to be in relationship with each of us.

When the Author of the Bible lives inside of us, He enables the Book to come alive within us. It's like being a gold miner; nugget by nugget, we grow as we apply His Word in our lives. This is a lifelong process: hearing God, receiving impressions from Him, and working these thoughts out in our mind so that they become a part of our daily walk.

Walking in the Spirit involves the process of renewing the mind. As the mind is renewed, the Holy Spirit speaks through the Word of God. As our walk becomes steadier, verses in the Bible will "jump out" or "come alive"–they just make sense! When this happens, we have the choice to act upon those verses–putting what we know into practice and action. That is evidence of the Holy Spirit's filling, and that is what walking in the Spirit looks like.

Walking in the Spirit means learning to read the Bible with expectation. Expect that God is going to communicate with you in everyday affairs. He is interested in every little detail and in everything I do. He will faithfully speak through His Word, and he will remain personal! The Holy Spirit is our Guide and Teacher–He walks us through every step of the day. He can speak through His Word, and often also speaks through others.

CHALLENGE:

The little foxes ruin the vine.
It does not require a huge negative to bring ruin. In other words, the negative could be something like a small lie, but a small lie can bring huge ruin into a person's life.
Pray for God to reveal any areas you may need to have changed.
Face the truth, and then deal with it, replacing the negative with a positive truth from the Word.
Prayer is a powerful weapon and salve!

Lies and untruths in my life (about God, others, and myself):

_____

_____

_____

_____

Positive truth from God's word:

_____

_____

_____

_____

CHAPTER 11
EXTENDING FORGIVENESS

"Be kind to one another, tender-hearted, forgiving one another, as God in Christ forgave you."
~ Apostle Paul (Eph 4:32)

Forgiveness is a willful choice. One of the misguided myths about forgiveness that most of us have adopted is that people think that forgiveness is a feeling. "If I don't feel it, it's not real – it's fake." Forgiveness is not a feeling; it's a choice; it's an act of the will. As I forgive, I am freed, and when I am freed, the person who is or has offended can also be freed.

Forgiveness is an abstract word

We think in pictures. When you hear the word "dog," we picture a dog rather than seeing D-O-G. Therefore we need to identify with the pictures that God has given us.

Please note the imagery from these passages:

Isaiah 1:18

_____

Isaiah 44:22

_____

Psalm 103:11-12

_____

Micah 7:19

_____

Forgiveness is a major step that changes a negative habit pattern to a positive habit pattern. When one operates in forgiveness, one takes full responsibility for one's attitudes, feelings, and behaviors. It is fairly common to hear people say, "You make me so...!"

No one can make so feel anything!

People as a rule do not want to own their responses and reactions. By saying something like this, one is in essence giving another person the power to control one's emotions. A better way to put it would be to say, "When you do _____, I feel _____. I haven't learned how to handle that yet."

Then one is being responsible. If somebody is "making you mad", then you are saying that you cannot do anything about it. But by acknowledging that you don't know how to handle something, you are taking responsibility and admitting that there is something you can do about it.

Forgiveness is refusing to sit in the seat of judgment and actually receiving forgiveness for having judged. Another way to say "receiving forgiveness" is repenting. Forgiveness is not human; it's divine. Forgiveness is beyond what natural man can comprehend or understand. It is a supernatural act that takes practice to perfect.

Consequences of Unforgiveness

Christians who choose not to forgive experience two consequences (among others):

1. The unforgiving Christian's prayers seem like they are "dead." Often, this person does not experience feeling alive, and this person is often not active in walking out their faith.

2. When a Christian is unforgiving, Christ's life is essentially choked out, distorting the Christian's image of God.

A real example:
For instance, before I received forgiveness for perfectionism, my view of God was that He was a harsh judge. My view of Him was distorted, and I was unable to see Him as a Friend, or as one who forgives and has compassion.

The result of these consequences is that unforgiveness often hinders God's work in our lives! It does not change his love for us or our standing in Christ, but it gives the enemy a foothold and we create a barrier in our minds, thus hardening our hearts. Living in unforgiveness creates a separation in our experience of God's love. Scripture confirms this principal in the following passages:

Psalm 66:18

_____

Isaiah 59:1&2

_____

Mark 11:25&26

_____

Matthew 6:12

_____

1 John 1:6-9

_____

WE MUST <u>CHOOSE</u> TO *EXTEND* FORGIVENESS!!

When we do not *extend* forgiveness, we will likely experience anger, resentment, self-pity, bitterness, depression, and jealousy.
We have seen previously how emotions can impact us physically — to the point of physical sickness.

If harboring unforgiveness has the potential to create the above emotions, and if those emotions open the doors of hurt and trauma, it is reasonable to say that unforgiveness can lead to many physical ailments. Extending forgiveness means "to let go."

Extending forgiveness does not require that you actually physically go to the person. Circumstances may be such that you may not be able to if they are dead, in an unknown location, or contact is unsafe. The key is becoming free, and verbalization solidifies the extension of forgiveness.

No situation or problem in life will ever *leave* you the same way it *finds* you. Life is, and will continue to be, full of circumstances that are good and bad. There are really only two options: one can either become *bitter* or *better*. When one chooses to become better, one chooses to grow through the circumstance.

CHALLENGE:

A practical method of working through forgiveness is to write everything out.
Writing it out provides finality to the issue at hand. When you choose to grant or extend forgiveness, write it out and then verbalize it for emphasis.
I choose to forgive you, _____, for _____.

Name the person, and name the sin or offense, and *choose* to let it go.
By doing this, it's like you have taken the backpack off of your hook, and placed it onto God's hook, allowing him to deal with that individual and bring about the changes needed in that person's life.
It's amazing what great things come out of this seemingly little step!

_____

_____

_____

_____

_____

CHAPTER 12

RECEIVING FORGIVENESS

But to all who believed him and accepted him, he gave the right to become children of God
John 1:12

RECEIVE - verb (mainly transitive)

1. to take (something offered) into one's hand or possession

2. to have (an honour, blessing, etc) bestowed

3. to accept delivery or transmission of (a letter, telephone call, etc)

When we do not *receive* forgiveness, we will likely experience a sense of worthlessness, rebellion, denial, a critical spirit, withdrawal, guilt, shame, blame, and a tendency towards perfectionism. Have you ever caught yourself "role-playing" a conversation?

Perhaps you've said something like, "She'd say...and then I'd say...and then she'd say...and then..." In other words, you've spent valuable time rehearsing and nursing all sorts of predictions. The other type of role-play that often occurs when one has not received forgiveness is, "If I just do everything perfect, then I'll be ok..."

You are only going to *experience* God's forgiveness to the level that you have *extended* and *received* forgiveness. Your experience of God's forgiveness towards you relates directly to how willing you are to forgive those who have offended you. It also relates to your willingness to acknowledge the areas where you may have offended someone and are in need of forgiveness.

Read Luke 7:39-50 and take note of the Pharisees' attitude compared to Jesus:

_____

_____

If you are basically a "good" person, you may struggle with showing compassion and mercy – because you have had very little need to be shown compassion or mercy. In Luke 7, the woman fell weeping at Jesus' feet and washed his feet with expensive perfume and her hair.

The Pharisees judged her for sins they perhaps had not committed. They, in their human logic, thought that if Jesus knew who she was, he would never have allowed her to touch him. Jesus, whose divinity defied human logic, stated in verse 47: *"For this reason I say to you, her sins, which are many, have been forgiven, for she loved much; but he who is forgiven little, loves little."*

If you have had a difficult life, you most likely have acquired the capacity to love at a deeper level than those who have not suffered like you. Your compassion and mercy will be greater because you have actually walked and lived through being on the receiving end of compassion and mercy.

Perhaps the Pharisees were not able to extend forgiveness because they were not ready to receive the love and forgiveness that Christ was bringing to the world. What areas/types of people do you struggle with having mercy and compassion for? Ask God to show you the root of this issue.

_____

_____

Forgiveness is both *critical* and *progressive*. It is critical in that we each need to recognize our personal *need* to forgive. No one is exempt. It is progressive in that our feelings are not going to change immediately, but will rather progress along with time. Emotions take time to catch up with our will.

You may not *feel* like you forgave, but if you verbalized it, then you did! Remember, forgiveness is a choice, and it is divine. It may not make sense, humanly speaking, but God is faithful, and is in the business of bringing about freedom. You do your part, and forgive, and He'll do his part, and bring your emotions around.

Hebrews 5:14 says: *But solid food is for the mature, who because of practice have **their senses trained** to discern good and evil.* As we walk in the light, our senses are trained. Our emotions catch up through the progressive process. This happens as walking in the light becomes a way of life.

CHALLENGE:

Go back to the pictures that God gives us for forgiveness and begin to identify with one or all of them.

Isaiah 1:18   Isaiah 44:22
Psalm 103:11-12   Micah 7:19

Begin to practice this in your life when you are living under condemnation, under guilt, not in freedom or peace.

Visualize the picture you identify with and treasure it in your heart.

As you practice this it will become automatic and you will learn to walk in Abundant Life. The enemy will no longer be able to rob, steal and destroy. (John 10:10) but you will walk in the Kingdom of God, which is abundance of righteousness, peace and joy. (Romans 14:17)

For further information and to ask Peter for a seminar or speaking engagement:

Please call

Peter J. Dahl

4225 Townline Road
Abbotsford, BC V4X 1Y7

tel: 604 308.3626
email: phd@tdfa.net

About the Author

Peter was born into a loving Christian family, number 4 of 9 children, raised on a farm where he learned the work ethic. Peter grew up with a speech impediment which caused him to feel insecure, insignificant, and not do well in school. Peter's concept of God was wrong; he thought he had to be good enough and keep the rules to be accepted by God.

Trying hard till sixteen, he tuned God out, quit school, went to work to make millions. He married his high school sweetheart, Heidi, very young. At twenty-six, they faced a crisis Heidi & Peter had agreed every little boy should go to Sunday School. Heidi went, but Peter stayed home to watch his N.F.L. games. Heidi received Christ and was going to be baptized. Peter threatened her that the day she got baptized, he would divorce her.

Secretly he had started reading the Bible. He came across Rev. 3:20. Peter states: "God was standing at the door of my life and wanting to be my friend. That startled me. Facing the crisis of loosing my family, afraid, lonely, I listened to a Hank Snow song called, "What then," where he asked the questions, 'When you've spent your last dollar, crowd seeking pleasure gone home, judge of the earth says closed for the night, what then?'

"Back to my mind came the thought that the creator of the universe wanted to be my friend, so as an act of my will, I invited Him (Jesus)in. I was saved, and water baptized the following Sunday with my wife. We rebuilt our family.

"Then I began my search for the abundant life that Christ offered. It was a long joyful journey. My heart's desire was to influence as many people as possible to receive Christ and become disciples. This took me to crisis line where I spent 19 years with Burden Bearers of Canada, starting offices throughout British Columbia and Alberta.

"I always worked by appointment and didn't charge a fee. Freely you have received, freely give."

Peter has a farming and business background. At one point he was the chairman of a public mining exploration company.

Peter has traveled much of the world on business and mission trips and seen good fruit. He enjoys his family and continues to help people find Christ and become disciples.

The principles in the study have been used in Peter's office for 35 years with very satisfying results and we trust you will receive the same results and experience God's goodness and abundance.

Peter and Heidi have been married 55 years, and have 5 sons, 5 daughters-in-law and 15 grandchildren.

To contact the publisher:

HeartBeat Productions Inc.

Box 633

Abbotsford, BC Canada V2T 6Z8

email: info@heartbeat1.com

604.852.3769

Made in the USA
Middletown, DE
07 November 2019